A Survival Kit for the Substitute & New Teacher

Your Blueprint to Having a Successful Day

Jennifer Gaither

JenRod Publishing

A Survival Kit for the Substitute and New Teacher: Your Blueprint to Having a Successful Day

Copyright © 1998 by Jennifer Gaither

For information or to contact the author, address correspondence to:

JenRod Publishing
6107 Hopeton Avenue, Baltimore, MD 21215
Telephone (410)-358-3360

Library of Congress Catalog Card Number: Pending

Gaither, Jennifer,
 A Survival Kit for the Substitute and New Teacher
 1. Education 2. Teacher guide 3. Student motivation 4. Teacher motivation

ISBN: 0-9664154-0-X

A percentage of the proceeds from the sale of this book will be donated to the Coppin State College Scholarship Fund.

First Edition
5 4 3 2 1

Dedication

This book is dedicated to all new educators, practice teachers, and substitute teachers who are committed to the education of our children and desire to see them reach their potential.

I pray that the essence of this book will penetrate their hearts, for it was sown in love and sincerity, so that it will reap a harvest of peace and respect.

Acknowledgments

Special thanks to the Hazelwood Middle School 1996-97 school year Seventh and Eighth grade classes who worked so diligently to create the many games and puzzles.

Many thanks to Anna Westerman, Kiera Edwards, and Usha Tyson who sorted through hundreds of pieces of materials.

Special thanks to Brian Ray who typed and edited much of this material.

Table of Contents

Introduction

So you want to be a substitute teacher? Well, it's time to prepare for the task at hand. There are dozens of little urchins ready to unleash all of their energy and frustrations upon you. You, therefore, must be armed with a plan that will motivate, challenge, captivate, and bring peace to the classroom without revealing your tactics to them.

Simply put, this book is an array of ideas for the substitute to keep the children on target while providing a pleasant change of pace from the regular routine.

This book was divinely inspired and was birthed out of a need for our educational system to be uninterrupted by the absence of the regular teacher. It comes from a genuine love for children. These activities have worked for me, and I share them with you with the hope that they will boast your ability to effectually continue the learning process with our children.

This book will also assist the practice teacher and probationary teacher to get a handle on the control and discipline of a class. It is not designed to replace curriculum but to be used as a strategy to implement the curriculum in a creative way. These activities will motivate, captivate, and challenge your clients.

It is assumed by the children that you can't handle them, and that they will have their way. This book gives suggestions that will allow you more control and promise them more excitement than usual. Feel free to alter, add to, delete, or modify any activity to suit your needs at the time.

This survival kit is just what it says. When you enter into a classroom arena, you must bring a bag of tricks, gimmicks, puzzles, and games to capture the attention of the students and will prove, also, to be good listening, writing, and thinking skills.

Even though teachers leave plans, they are seldom carried out because of poor behavior. If the regular plans are carried out, the climate within the classroom is stiff and intimidating.

This book can be used in conjunction with a partial plan from the regular teacher or last minute hiring for the substitute. Every substitute or practice teacher enters the teaching arena with high expectations of doing a superb job only to be beaten down quickly by poor behavior. This survival kit will help those who go into the classroom trenches to do battle.

This book will arm and equip you to win the war.

What Are Your Motives?

Have you asked yourself this question? Why am I here? If the answer is to just pick up a pay check, you are in the wrong business.

The business of instructing children must be motivated from the heart. Caring for and loving children will enable you to rise above the common day obstacles.

If you are genuine, they'll know it. If you are sincere, they'll feel it. If the pay check is the main focus, they'll read that message too. Children can spot insecurity, lack of confidence, and a push over instantly.

If you love children, this book will provide you with strategies and techniques to capture the interest and sustain that interest for the duration of the lesson. This is a job that requires observation, preparation, organization, and dedication.

You Are Your Best Advocate— Sell Yourself!

Each individual has gifts and talents that they should utilize to captivate children. Use what you have or what you can do to enhance your relationship with children.

If you tap dance, bring your shoes and find a connection between that subject and tapping. I sing, so some lessons are sung. As I repeat a rule over and over, students begin to hum with a beat to my multi syllabic phrases.

If your talent is in art, actually draw and sketch something for them. This would be a good time to dust off the guitar and strum a tune. You are gifted in some way.

Bring your gift with you to share and watch the reaction. Children need to know they are special, and these activities help to convince them that you care.

Discipline

Good discipline is the essential key to producing success in the classroom. If you fail to gain control, you can look for some long frustrated days ahead.

Upon arrival to your school, always introduce yourself to the other teachers on the same grade level. Always ask if you can request help if necessary. The teachers on that level will already know your students and can be a source of assistance, if necessary.

If a child creates significant problems, move his/her seat. If necessary, repeat your actions with a stronger reprimand. The next step is to remove that child from your room to possibly another room in the vicinity, thereby having a time-out session away from the problem for 15-20 minutes.

Do not allow 1 or 2 children to create pandemonium for the entire class. Remove the source of the problem. If no teacher will assist you, then call for help in the office. The point is that you are in charge and must have control.

Make sure you secure phone numbers (from office) of all problem students and follow-up with a phone call. Be consistent. If you say you're going to call home, make sure you call home and address the problem.

You must not tolerate rebellious attitudes. Students must know that you mean business. The word will get around through the pipeline and eventually, poor behavior will be cut to a minimum.

Never carry a grudge against your students for their wrong doings. Start each day fresh with a new attitude. You may want to call on them first and reward them for raising their hand and not yelling out. Let them know that things are all right and be ready to praise them for their efforts.

The bottom line on discipline is, "When in doubt, check it out." It is better to ask a teacher rather than believe everything the children say because they do want to have their way.

Here is a word of caution. The bonding process takes time, and some students will rebel against your method until they understand your position and personality.

Never leave the school day with the students. Do not allow them to identify your car until you have established a good rapport with them. Some students may want to retaliate against you before you have bonded with them. This is true mainly at the middle school level.

You must earn their respect before they will trust you. Allow yourself time to show love, concern, and give them respect. Never hesitate to ask for divine wisdom in any given situation.

Materials

"To be forewarned is to be forearmed." This is a true statement.

- Always come prepared.

- Never lose 5-10 minutes searching for something which gives our little friends an opportunity to get off task.

- Be prepared.

- When you go to any assignment, make sure that you have a marker, masking tape, scissors, chalk, pencil, and pen.

- Never enter a classroom empty handed.

- Think upon these items as part of the job that belong in your survival kit along with this book.

• If this is the first day of a particular assignment, always arrive early to look over plans and scope the room to begin to identify things you can use that are already present.

• Bulletin boards may be helpful to identify units of study.

• Charts may be available from which you may collect subject vocabulary lists.

First Step

Even before you are hired, begin the taping of various shows. The first step that should be taken when accepting an assignment is to have the principal sign-up the VCR for you. This one step can alleviate many problems on the first day.

Be prepared to tape programs of every magnitude or topic over the summer or during breaks. This investment is an invaluable tool that will allow you more freedom to interact with students.

Children love animal tapes from the zoo or wildlife. Cable channels afford you the opportunity to tape freely on any topic. Of course, these tapes can be purchased. Organize your animal tapes into three categories:

- 1) Humorous tapes for all ages, but better for primary,

• 2) Informative tapes for all ages which give tons of facts or even tell stories by using animals as characters,

• 3) Aggressive tapes would be enjoyable for the middle school students and might include topics, such as sharks, lions, snakes, etc. This last grouping tends to be too overwhelming for younger children, but provides lots of action for more mature taste.

Stop the tapes from time to time to make sure everyone is participating and watching or to ask questions for students to predict the outcome. Always have an assignment related to the tape which will direct and guide their thinking.

The following are examples of some assignments:

• 1) Language Arts—List 10 facts you learned.

• 2) Connect the dots of an animal shape.

• 3) Draw a picture of the animal.

• 4) Have questions prepared for older students.

• 5) Encyclopedia Assignment—research more facts about a particular animal

The VCR activity can be used as a reward for students' cooperation, or as a motivating technique for them to work harder with you. Each situation has to be analyzed and evaluated as to how it will bring you the desired result.

A second taping activity would be TV comedies, such as *Andy Griffith, Lucy, Gomer Pyle, Dick Van Dyke, Mama's Family, What's Happening, The Cosby Show,* and other tasteful comedies. The older comedies will ensure proper language and themes. More contemporary comedies must be previewed to eliminate inappropriate language and topics. Again, be ready with a follow-up activity related to the topic.

A third taping activity would be sporting events. These tapes can range from boxing to the NBA or track and field. Some students may bring in their own Michael Jordan tapes and others. These prove to be quite motivating for incentives or rewards. Olympic competition will also be appropriate for all ages.

Yet a fourth taping activity would be that of the catastrophic type of TV documentary, or you may purchase them from television stations. Older students are enthralled to see nature appearing to be "out of control." This type of activity provides good writing follow-ups using the dictionary, encyclopedia, projects, drawings, or question and answer activity. Students will begin to have respect for natural occurrences.

It might appear to be a labor-some job to do the taping, but remember, you are building a survival kit which will contain hours of relief for you and enjoyment for the student. Remember, the first thing you do upon accepting the assignment is to have the principal sign you up for the VCR. You are now equipped with backup tapes if needed.

Puzzles

No survival kit would be complete without puzzles. There are many dollar stores and flea markets that have puzzles ranging from 25-100 pieces. These puzzles' sizes can be handled within a 10-20 minute activity for students ranging from primary to middle. Students can work cooperatively in small groups (5-6) for competition. Of course, you must be prepared to give prizes to the winners.

After the puzzles have been worked, talk about a list of strategies used to work these puzzles.

Some strategies would be:

- (1) edges first,

- (2) color patterns,

- (3) turn all pieces over, or

• (4) each person works a section.

Older students can graph qualities, while younger children can write a story about their picture.

There are also picture or word puzzles. You must determine which puzzle would be more appropriate for your age group (See puzzles). These puzzles are divided into several categories, and answers are provided.

Once students have gotten the hang of doing each type, allow them the opporunity to work cooperatively and independently to create their own puzzles. Be prepared to give prizes for the group or individuals who can work very fast. There will be another section on prizes further in the book.

Word Lists

Since vocabulary is so essential to the learning process, there are many things that you can do with 20 words. This list may be drawn for subject areas, spelling, holidays, safety, community helpers, school supplies, and character traits. I will show you what you can do with a list of words from primary, intermediate, and middle school levels.

Primary — Kindergarten to Grade Three

1. jacks	6. clay	11. doll
2. bike	7. rope	12. chair
3. ball	8. skates	13. game
4. marbles	9. checkers	14. paint
5. car	10. blue	15. blocks

Classification- Skill

- Long Vowels
- Short Vowels
- Inside toys
- Outside toys
- Soft

- Dangerous
- Partners
- Two Syllable
- Plural
- Singular

Intermediate (Grade Four and Grade Five)

1. newscaster
2. athlete
3. doctor
4. lawyer
5. teacher

6. artist
7. writer
8. engineer
9. vocalist
10. musician

Activities

- Alphabetize

- Number of Syllables

- Compound Word

- Root Words

- Which profession would you consider and why?

- Casual Dress

- Public Eye

- Using each word in a sentence

- Requires college?

Middle School

1. generous	7. intelligent
2. determined	8. patient
3. selfish	9. trustworthy
4. responsible	10. dishonest
5. loyal	11. liar
6. obedient	12. talkative

Activities

A. Alphabetize

B. Number of syllables

C. Positive

D. Negative

E. Which traits best describe you?

F. Parts of Speech

G. Write a synonym

H. Write the opposite.

I. Root word

J. Identify a smaller word inside of the bigger word?

As you see, it does not matter what the list is as long as the words relate to each other in some way. Sometimes, you are notified at the last minute. If you ever need time to collect other material, the word list will provide you with enough time to go through the lesson plans for the next activity.

Music

Primary students love nursery rhymes, such as *Twinkle, Twinkle Little Star, Little Jack Horner*, etc. Always arrive early to identify songs you would want to play. If you can sing, teaching a song is quite motivational.

Songs which teach numbers, letters, or shapes will keep a class spellbound. You could select a student who is willing to lead the class in a favorite song too.

If no lyrics are available, or you are unable to sing, music that is dramatic or expressive is a sure winner. Children can march, skip, or hop to the beat. At that point, body movement can change into a physical aerobics activity. By this time, they will be ready to sit and listen to a story.

Intermediate

The children at this level are more sophisticated and need different types of gimmicks. Search the library, classical music stores, primary classes in your school, or the music teacher.

You need to look for different types of music, such as circus, ballet, suspenseful, happy times, or intensifying music that is mood setting and creates an atmosphere. Play the music and then ask the students to write a story or a list of words based upon the changes in the music. They could also create a vocabulary list based upon the story. Each child would then share their results. Many topics will be repeated.

A graph could be made of the topics for each selection played to compare numbers with the same topics. The activity could also be successful with middle school students by requiring a short story to be written.

Middle School

Set your radio dial to the hippest station and record several decent rap songs, club songs, and love songs. This must be closely scrutinized as not to be vulgar or provocative. Select the most tasteful songs with a positive message.

These songs could be used for students to paraphrase, interpret, and define the language. This activity can also be motivation for children to complete other activities. If they complete their work, you could as an added bonus ask them to show you a few steps (2-3 minutes).

Don't ever let them override you, but use this ploy to control them. You should never just ask the class to dance or let the activity go on for an half an hour. Remember, you are in charge. Your ultimate goal is to have order, challenge their thinking, and allow the learning process to flow.

Storytelling

This activity is great for all ages. Children love for you to read to them. If you can read dramatically and cause the story to become alive, the attention of every child will be captivated.

For younger children any fairy tale will suffice. The intermediate love *Charlotte's Web, Old Yeller, Tom Sawyer,* and *Treasure Island.* When you read to this age group, make sure you pause from time to time to ask questions, or make predications which can challenge their thinking.

Middle school students enjoy books, such as *The Call of the Wild, Fahrenheit 451, The Autobiography of Miss Jane Pittman, Gifted Hands,* and any sequels. A trip to the library can produce the latest exciting novels.

The point is, the more you put yourself into the activity, the more children will beg you to read to them.

- Previewing a chapter or book ahead of time will allow you to be prepared with an activity to enhance your story, such as word search puzzles, using characters and vocabulary from the book.

- Having each student draw his/her rendition of a scene from the story can be another activity.

- Having a vocabulary list prepared will allow you to further promote the story.

- Children need to see activities connected and related to them.

- Identifying characters from the story with similar character traits of your students will provide another opportunity for the students to see themselves in unique situations.

Prizes

It's time to pay up! There are oodles of prizes and reward systems that will thrill children and make them appreciate the activities you have presented to them. Feel free to add to, substitute, alter, or change these rewards to enable you to captivate your clientele.

Primary

• Balloons can be purchased by the hundreds very cheaply at outlets, dollar stores, or warehouses.

• Fast food stores often have free giveaways, and you and your friend can collect these hats, toys, or puzzles and stash them away.

• Prizes from cereal boxes can also be collected for future prizes.

• There are other prizes that can be recycled such as wearing a special badge or button for a day. This is a prestigious award, and younger children love it.

• An award for the primary child can also be a special activity such as painting, drawing, working with clay, playing with a special game, working puzzles, or even doing a special job.

Intermediate

• For the intermediate classes, a five minute game activity is a welcomed relief from the rigors of work or for good behavior. The students already know the games. (i.e., 7-up, Hangman, King vs. Queen) All you do is pick captains or leaders to initiate the games.

• The TV/VCR can also be used as a reward for positive behavior.

• Listening to a story or mystery on cassette is also a welcomed treat.

• Older children would enjoy a sports video or a game of basketball in the gym (if available).

Here is a word of caution on taking students from the classroom. You should only use this reward method when students have shown a respect for your presence and position. If they cannot be controlled in the classroom, you will not control them in the open space of a gym or outdoors. The rule is to keep them contained until they are controlled.

• A final reward could be edible snacks.
  Pretzels are cheap and healthier.
  Fruit snacks would also be enjoyable.
  Cheese crackers or raisins and nuts are good also.
  Occasionally, a cookie or candy treat can be given.

The following are ideas that can be used to generate competition, excitement, rewards, or a teaching tool. They can be used as drills, thinking skills, motivators, or creative assignments. They are to be used as you desire.

Feel free to alter, add to, or delete in any way that will assist you in establishing or maintaining control. They should not be used as just busy work, but as tools to get students to want to work. All of the following activities were created by students. Your children can do the same. They have the ability. They just need to be shown how.

Good luck!

One Syllable Rhyming Jokes

What do you call . . .

1) the place where bees live?
2) a sad plant?
3) a footie dance?
4) a footie that tells time?
5) a piece of wood that does nothing?
6) a furry animal that eats too much?
7) a dark animal that crawls?
8) a piece of bread that you put in the oven?
9) a male action figure?
10) a meowing animal that is overweight?
11) a positive piece of the sky?
12) a noisy group?
13) windy money?
14) clothes for seats?
15) a body of water that bends for miles?

16) a sleeping brain?
17) a chicken that lives in a coop?
18) an impolite surfer?
19) a star that has a good time?
20) an evening candle?
21) a doll that wears metal?
22) a wealthy hen?
23) a depressed father?
24) a cleaning utensil that dances?
25) an appetizer for lake trout?
26) a fly in your cup?
27) a tiny bug that is ill?
28) an insect that is stuck to your dessert?
29) an eaten apple that has no money?
30) happy play things?
31) a market that puts you to sleep?
32) letters that have been arrested?
33) a seasonal party?

1) bee tree
2) grief leaf
3) sock rock
4) sock clock
5) bored board
6) dog hog
7) black cat
8) roast toast
9) boy toy
10) fat cat
11) proud cloud
12) loud crowd

13) air fair
14) chair ware
15) tall falls
16) bed head
17) hen pen
18) rude dude
19) fun sun
20) night light
21) tin Ken
22) rich chick
23) sad dad
24) mop hop

25) fish dish
26) bug mug
27) sick tick
28) fly pie
29) poor core
30) toy joy
31) store bore
32) jail mail
33) spring fling

Answers:

Two Syllable Rhyming Jokes

What do you call . . .

1) an emotion that hits?

2) a sweet rabbit?

3) a candy that smiles?

4) a rabbit that tells jokes?

5) a man who shoots arrows in the wall?

6) a friend that is crazy?

7) a smelly finger?

8) a stinky gorilla?

9) a smart cat?

10) a mother actress?

11) a lobster that is fat?

12) a person that tells on a thief?

13) a rabbit that is messy?

14) a large sad cat?

7) stinky pinky	14) crying lion
6) nutty buddy	13) sloppy hoppy
5) stupid cupid	12) stealer squealer
4) funny bunny	11) flabby crabby
3) laffy taffy	10) drama mama
2) honey bunny	9) witty kitty
1) happy slappy	8) funky monkey

Answers:

1)   Tim.
     Tim who?
     Timber.

2)   Jimmy.
     Jimmy who?
Jimmy cracked corn, and I don't care.

3)   Linda.
     Linda who?
     Linda me some money.

4)   Art.
     Art who?
   Aren't you going to open the door?

5)   Anita.
     Anita who?
     Anita a pencil.

Knock, Knock!
Who's There?

6) Lettuce.
Lettuce who?
Lettuce in.

7) Phillip.
Phillip who?
Phillip your tank.

8) Ad.
Ad who?
Adverbs to your list.

9) Knauer.
Knauer who?
Knauer is the time.

10) Phillip.
Phillip who?
Phillip my glass with juice.

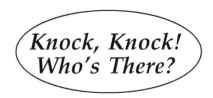

*Knock, Knock!
Who's There?*

11)   Robert.
      Robert who?
      I'm going to Rob Bert of his candy.

12)   Mailena.
      Mailena who?
      May Lena borrow a pencil?

13)   Justin.
      Justin who?
      Just in a minute.

14)   I'm a.
      I'm a who?
      I'm a gonna get you.

15)   Lisa.
      Lisa who?
      Lisa to me carefully.

Knock, Knock! Who's There?

16) Hill.
    Hill who?
    He'll buy us some candy.

17) Shoe.
    Shoe who?
    Shoe fly don't bother me.

18) He'll.
    He'll who?
He'll be coming round the mountain.

19) Comma.
    Comma who?
    Comma inside.

20) Little Old Lady.
    Little Old Lady who?
    I didn't know you could yodel.

*Knock, Knock!
Who's There?*

21)   Carla.
      Carla who?
      Carla back.

22)   Danielle.
      Danielle who?
      Danielle's at me!

23)   Cara.
      Cara who?
      I cara for you.

24)   Itch.
      Itch who?
      Bless you.

25)   Who?
      Who who?
      You sound like an owl.

Knock, Knock! Who's There?

26) Alisha.
     Alisha who?
     Alisha can do is let me do it.

Balloon Games

Mostly for fun . . .

1) •Whoever makes the best balloon face wins.

2) •Put a message in the balloon and another person has to do it.

3) •Put your name in a balloon with 9 other people, blow them up, scramble them, and then, find your name. *First 3 to finish win.*

4) •Sit on the balloon and try not to pop it.

5) •Put face descriptions on some cards. Have some kids pick a card and make that face on the balloon. *Then, have them judged.*

6) •Write some equations on a card, and put them in the balloon. Write the answer of them on the board. One person at a time will pop the balloon, read the equation, and match it with the answer on the board.

7) •Determine who can pop the most balloons in 30 seconds.

8) •Determine who can blow up the biggest balloon.

9) •Blow up a balloon. Then, pass it around in a circle while music plays. When the music stops, the person with the balloon is out.

10) •Pick a card with a word describing a person's face. Have a student or group draw the faces on balloons within thirty seconds, and have the class judge the results.

11) •Stick a math problem in some balloons. Then, pop the balloons, and if the students answer correctly, they get points for their table or team.

12) •You have a colorful assortment of balloons and the first letter of the color. The students name as many words as possible to see who can name more words.

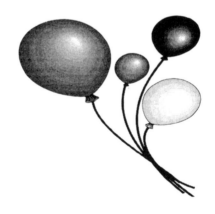

Line Games

For Social Studies Classes:

1)   •The girls and the boys make two separate lines.

•Each team names states and their capitals.

•Whoever names the most wins.

2)   •Divide the students into two groups.

•Have a bell in front of each line.

•Name a city.

•Whoever hits the bell first and names the right state, gets a point.

3)   •Divide the students into two lines (boys versus girls).

•You call west, east, north, <u>and</u> south after telling the directions.

•The direction you call is the direction they have to turn.

4)   •The students get in two lines.
        •The teacher names a continent.
        •A student on each side must name 2 states or 2 countries.

For Spelling or Social Studies Classes:

5)   •Make two lines.
        •Each person has to spell a state.
        •If they get it right, they go to the end of the line.
        •If they get it wrong, they have to go to their seat.

For Spelling Class:

6)   •Two teams line up.
        •They have a spelling bee.
        •The team that wins gets a treat.

For Mathematics Class:

7) •Divide the students into two lines.

•Give each person a different number.

•The first person in line multiplies the number by two.

•Continue the game in this way, and the first line to finish wins.

8) •Line up the children.

•Have them answer time factors.

•If you know the answer is wrong, the child goes back to their seat.

•If it is right, they go to the back of the line.

Racing Games

For Social Studies class:

1)　•Have two maps at the front of the room with 2 lines of children (5-6).

　　•Have each student circle the states in chalk listed on the board.

　　•The first team to finish wins.

2)　•A boy and girl go up to the board where the map should be placed.

　　•The teacher will name a state, and the first person to find it wins.

3)　•Students are equally split up into 4 groups.

•Each group has to write as many presidents as possible.

•The group that wins gets a treat.

4)   •Divide the students into 2 groups, boys versus girls.

•When the teacher says a city, the children take turns guessing the state.

•Whoever has the most points wins.

5)   •Whoever can give the capital of a state or city in a state wins.

For Language Arts (Spelling, Reading, etc.)

6)   •There will be two lines with the girls against the boys.

•The teacher will pick a letter, and each child

will have 10 seconds to say 5 words that begin with that letter.

7)   •Make three teams.

•Give all of the teams a scrambled word.

•Whoever has the correct answer first receives a point for his/her team.

8)   •Divide the students into teams.

•Give them a letter.
Give the children 5 minutes to make up as many words as possible beginning with that letter.

9)   •Select a consonant blend.
•Give each student 2 minutes to write as many words beginning with that blend as possible.

•(Ex. If you give the students *bl*, possible responses might be *black, blue,* <u>and</u> *blend*.)

10)   •The teacher makes two even lines.

•Then, he/she asks the students a question, and then they go to the back of the line after answering it.

•Whichever line finishes answering questions first wins.

11)   •Divide the children into groups of four (boys versus girls).

•Have words with definitions taped to the board (6).

•The group that matches the words with their definitions wins.

12)   •In 60 seconds, who can come up with

the most verbs, prepositions, pronouns, adjectives, adverbs, synonyms, antonyms, <u>and</u> homonyms (3 or 4 students).

For Mathematics class:

13)   •This is a counting game.

•How many consecutive numbers can you count to 100 in 60 seconds?

14)   •Pick 6-8 children for each team.

•Assign the same number to each child on each team.

•Place a ball in the center of the room.

•Two students from each team are selected with the same number.

•Call out that number, and two students run out and try to get the ball.

•Whoever gets the ball first has to do an addition problem.

•Whichever team gets the most points wins.

15)   •Write a number problem (one or two operations), and give 5 seconds to respond.

Can You Guess These Products?

Below, there are slogans <u>or</u> clues that are commonly used when associating with a product. Using the clues below, can you identify the product?

- •1) Not going anywhere for a while
- •2) Just do it!
- •3) Have it your way

- •4) Bet you can't eat just one
- •5) Once you pop, you can't stop.
- •6) It does a body good.

- •7) The quicker-picker-upper
- •8) What would you do for a _____ bar?
- •9) I got the blue boy blues.

- 10) Best part of waking up . . .
- 11) Bite the burst
- 12) The real thing

- 13) Unlock the magic
- 14) Where's the cream filling?
- 15) The candy with double letters

- 16) Happy cowboy
- 17) Nest T
- 18) How do you like your _____?

- 19) Twisty candy
- 20) A laughy candy
- 21) Time out

- 22) Sometimes you feel like a nut . . .
- 23) Time, servant
- 24) $100,000

- 25) Give me a break
- 26) Taste the rainbow
- 27) Galaxy

?

- 28) 1,000 chips
- 29) RED
- 30) Uncola

- 31) Slippery finders
- 32) 3 heros
- 33) Her-she

- 34) Just for the taste of it
- 35) Mint/mint
- 36) Slam the dew

- 37) Crave the wave
- 38) Yum yum gum
- 39) This street sign goes up to five

- 40) I can't remember it
- 41) Hills of fun
- 42) Famous author

- 43) King of baseball
- 44) A ball in flames
- 45) A lot of "goods"

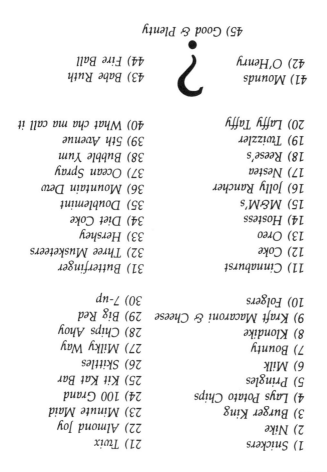

1) Snickers
2) Nike
3) Burger King
4) Lays Potato Chips
5) Pringles
6) Milk
7) Bounty
8) Klondike
9) Kraft Macaroni & Cheese
10) Folgers
11) Cinnabunst
12) Coke
13) Oreo
14) Hostess
15) M&M's
16) Jolly Rancher
17) Nestea
18) Reese's
19) Twizzler
20) Laffy Taffy
21) Twix
22) Almond Joy
23) Minute Maid
24) 100 Grand
25) Kit Kat Bar
26) Skittles
27) Milky Way
28) Chips Ahoy
29) Big Red
30) 7-up
31) Butterfinger
32) Three Musketeers
33) Hershey
34) Diet Coke
35) Doublemint
36) Mountain Dew
37) Ocean Spray
38) Bubble Yum
39) 5th Avenue
40) What cha ma call it
41) Mounds
42) O'Henry
43) Babe Ruth
44) Fire Ball
45) Good & Plenty

Word List— Parts of Speech

Nouns					
ape	boy	comb	dog	elf	fan
ace	booth	cat	doctor	elephant	foot
art	baby	cage	dish	egg	forehead
animal	ball	cake	door	elk	finger
angel	bomb	couch	dimple	earring	faucet
gate	hachet	ice	joke	kite	lamp
gum	house	igloo	jug	kitten	lake
goat	horse	iron	jumper	kangaroo	lion
ginger	hamper	island	junk	kilt	licorice
gift	hamburger	indigo	jelly	king	lamb

Nouns

mitten	niece	octopus	paint	queen	rope
milk	newt	orange	peach	quilt	robber
mouse	notes	ocean	paper	question	rock
monkey	nostril	oven	pancake	quarry	rabbit
magazine	name	oxen	possum	quaker	rocket
snake	title	uniform	vine	whole	yarn
snapper	tooth	unicorn	vein	watermelon	yellow
snail	tulip	urchin	violin	watch	yard
slug	toilet	ulcer	violet	wind	year
slush	table	umbrella	voice	wasp	yam
	x-ray	zipper	zebra	zoo	

Verbs

awake	bend	call	do	eat	fist
arise	break	cut	dip	earn	fight
ate	bring	carry	darn	equal	flip
act	bounce	can	dash	evaluate	forsake
arrive	brand	collect	dim	elect	freeze
grill	hop	insert	jump	kick	lick
give	hang	insure	jog	keep	love
gain	hide	invite	jingle	kiss	laugh
go	holler	irritate	justify	kneel	leak
glow	hit	invest	judge	knock	limp

Verbs

move	need	open	play	qualify	ram
make	nudge	overtake	punch	question	reach
massage	nick	outsmart	pledge	quit	rip
mix	nourish	orate	plead	quote	rain
match	narrate	offer	pluck	quarrel	rush
stomp	talk	use	visit	walk	yell
stash	touch	untie	voice	waste	yank
snip	type	unite	visualize	whip	yap
snap	take	understand	victimize	win	yield
sneak	tip	uncover	view	wake	yodel
	zap	zero	zoom		

Vocabulary For Various Subjects

Mathematics

addition	subtraction	multiplication	division	equal
addend	sum	quotient	algebra	fractions
decimals	facts	graphs	percentage	reduce
currency	number	whole	count	facts

Science

chemistry	atoms	forest	microscope	chemicals
nuclear	electrons	gas	scientist	solar system
planet	galaxy	animal	universe	earth
atmosphere	volcano	flower	root	stem

You Have Got To Have The Tools

Vocabulary For Various Subjects

Social Studies

civil	war	map	country	rights
globe	continent	colony	states	bill
island	bay	peninsula	law	veto
government	sea	ocean	president	judge

Reading/Literature

story	plot	setting	topic	opposition
characters	climax	resolution	paragraph	context
syllables	blends	synonyms	predict	details
homonyms	antonyms	main idea	conclusion	phonics

You Have Got To Have The Tools

Picture Word Puzzles
(Set I)

1) + run

2) *(clock with arrows)*

3) pilf

4) *(person with baseball)*

5) _____ under

6) J+

Picture Word Puzzles
(Set II)

1)	2)	3)
+ **butter**	**B4UGO**	**4U2CONLY**
4)	**H A I R**	**FAST→**

Picture Word Puzzles
(Set III)

1) HISTORY HISTORY HISTORY HISTORY

2) THINK

3) AIR

4) FOOT + + ER

5) BLOUSE

6) +

Picture Word Puzzles
(Set IV)

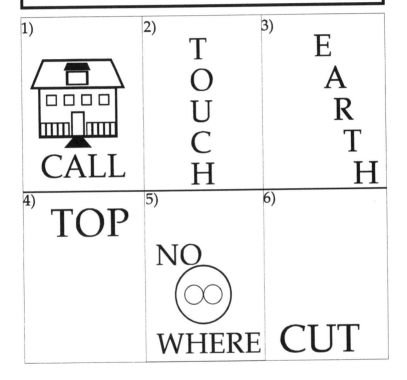

1)

2) TOUCH

3) EARTH

4) TOP

5) NO WHERE

6) CUT

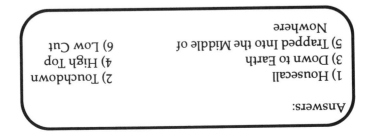

Picture Word Puzzles
(Set V)

1)

2)

3)

+ SHOE

4)

BE

- - - - -

TIME

5)

FIVE

6)

LAW

Picture Word Puzzles
(Set VI)

1) FLYING	2) TO TWO 2 TOO	3) MMMM M M M M
4) D R E S S	5) DOL LAR	6) 7 11 7 11 7 11 7 11 7 11

Picture Word Puzzles
(Set VII)

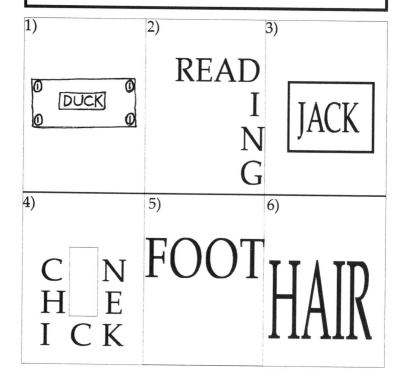

Picture Word Puzzles
(Set VIII)

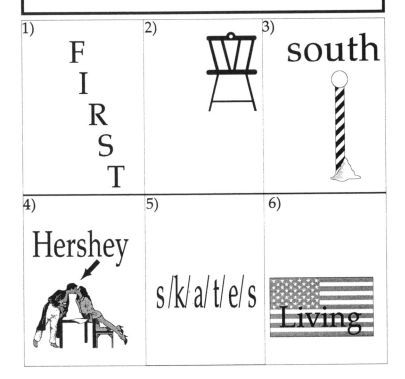

1) F I R S T

2) [high chair]

3) south

4) Hershey

5) s/k/a/t/e/s

6) Living

Picture Word Puzzles
(Set IX)

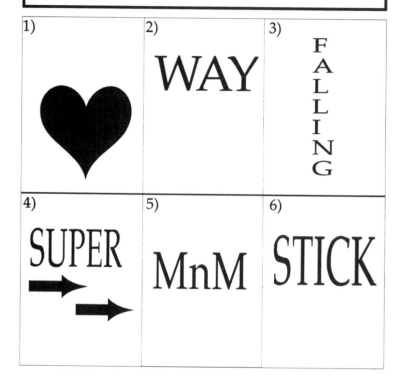

1)

2) WAY

3) FALLING

4) SUPER →→

5) MnM

6) STICK

Picture Word Puzzles
(Set X)

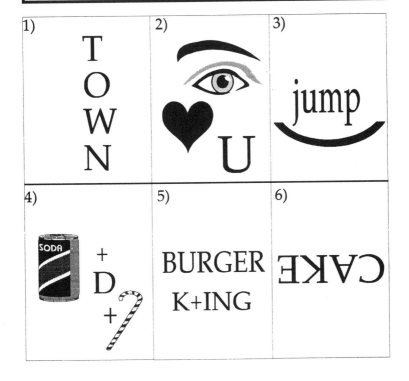

1)
T
O
W
N

2)
♥ U

3)
jump

4)
SODA
+ D
+

5)
BURGER
K+ING

6)
CAKE

Picture Word Puzzles
(Set XI)

1)

MINDED
MINDED

2)

YOU RIGHT

3)

S
O
U
T
H

4)

LOVE
———
HATE

Conclusion

This survival kit is designed to provide a variety of activities that will engage the learner in a continuous flow of education whenever the regular teacher is not present. It is also designed to assist the new teacher with ideas to get a handle on discipline and to help keep that learning spark alive.

Any activity used in part or in conjunction with your lesson is welcomed. This book is meant to be of assistance when other strategies have failed. It is not to replace curriculum, but it will bring life to any activity that you have created.

Feel free to apply any activity or strategy to your own subject, plans, or vocabulary lists.

About the Author

Jennifer Gaither was born Jennifer Lee Jones in Clarksburg, West Virginia, but she was raised and educated in the Baltimore City Public School System. She knew from early childhood that teaching would always be her career choice. Jennifer married and produced two children, a girl and a boy. Being a mother has enhanced and added to her positive approach to discipline.

Over the last twenty-five years, Jennifer has pursued her teaching career with zeal and enthusiasm. Her success and rapport with students has established her as a master teacher. Most of this success comes from using her God given abilities.

Mrs. Gaither has been named teacher representative on three occasions during her career from 1987, 1993, and 1995. Jennifer was also named **Middle School Teacher of the Year** for 1995 which is a highly selective honor. Her students fondly refer to her as *"Teacher #1."*

Mrs. Gaither's students have also acknowledged her leadership by nominating her for <u>Who's Who Among American Teachers</u> on three occasions.

Over the years, Jennifer has performed demonstration lessons for student teachers at the College of Notre Dame and Morgan State University. She is currently serving as a mentor teacher for Towson State University's Urban Teacher Candidate Program. Mrs. Gaither is an advocate of efficacy and maintains that students possess within themselves the power to succeed. The teacher's job is to find that spark and set the student on a hot pursuit to the pathway of knowledge.

After hearing so many horror stories from substitutes and new teachers, Jennifer was divinely inspired to write a handbook that would assist the "rookie" in motivation and discipline in the classroom. Anyone entering the classroom arena should not be without a "Survival Kit."

Jennifer Gaither is a graduate of Coppin State College with a B.S. degree in education and a Master's equivalent from Towson State University.

A percentage of the proceeds from the sale of this book will be donated to the Coppin State College Scholarship Fund.

Jennifer Gaither is available for seminar and workshop presentations upon request.

To contact the author:—
JenRod Publishing
6107 Hopeton Avenue
Baltimore, MD 21215
Telephone (410) 358-3360

Notes

Notes

Notes

Notes

DATE DUE

JUN 1 9 2000			
AUG 2 4 2000			